I0789030

Amazing Ocean Coloring Book

+ Active
Games
Mazes

For Kids
By
Nadya Hope

©Copyright 2020 by «Nadya Hope»

All rights reserved. No part of this publication or the information in it may be quoted from or reproduced in any form by means such as printing, scanning, photocoping or otherwise without prior written permission on the copyright holder.

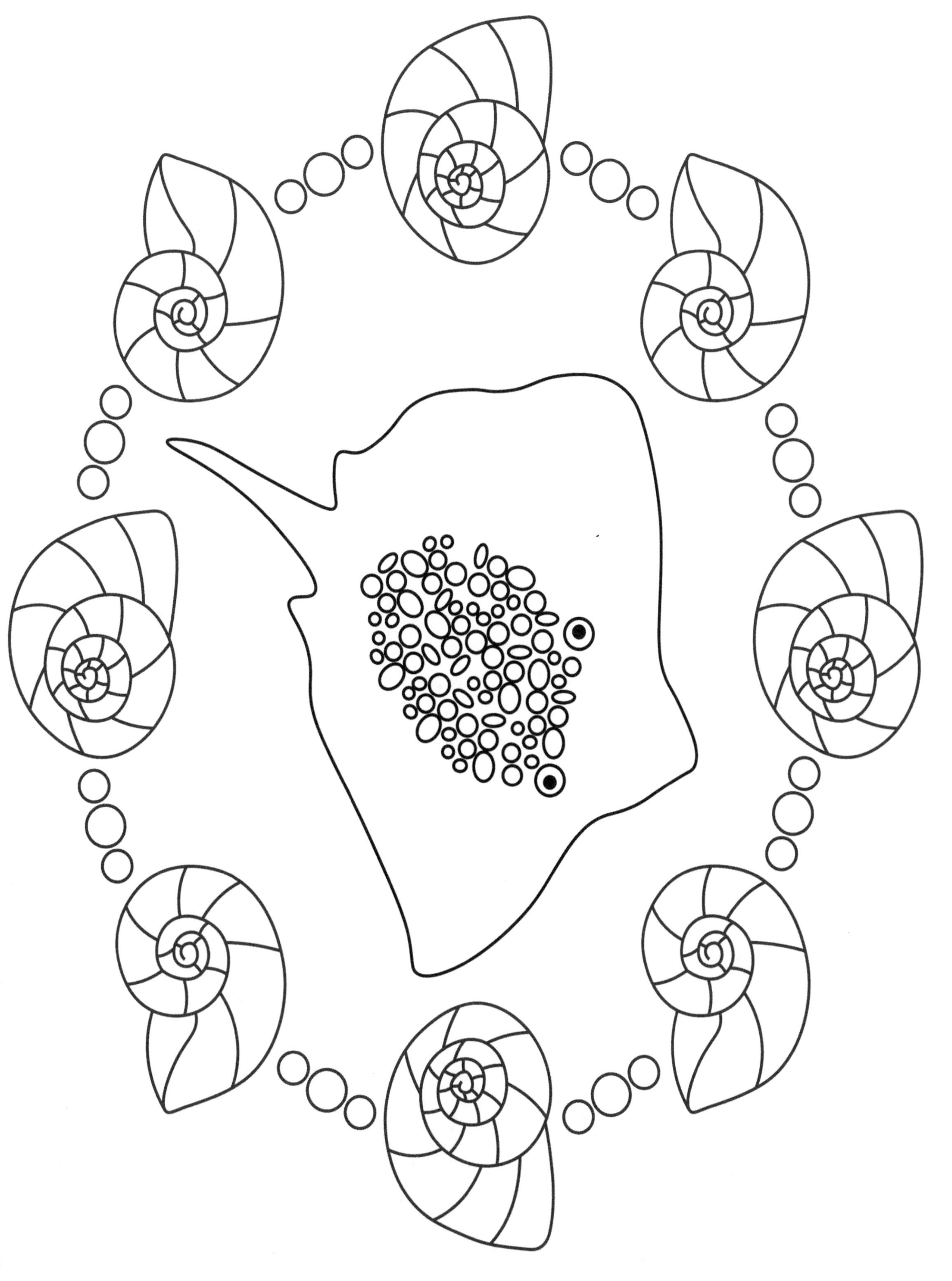

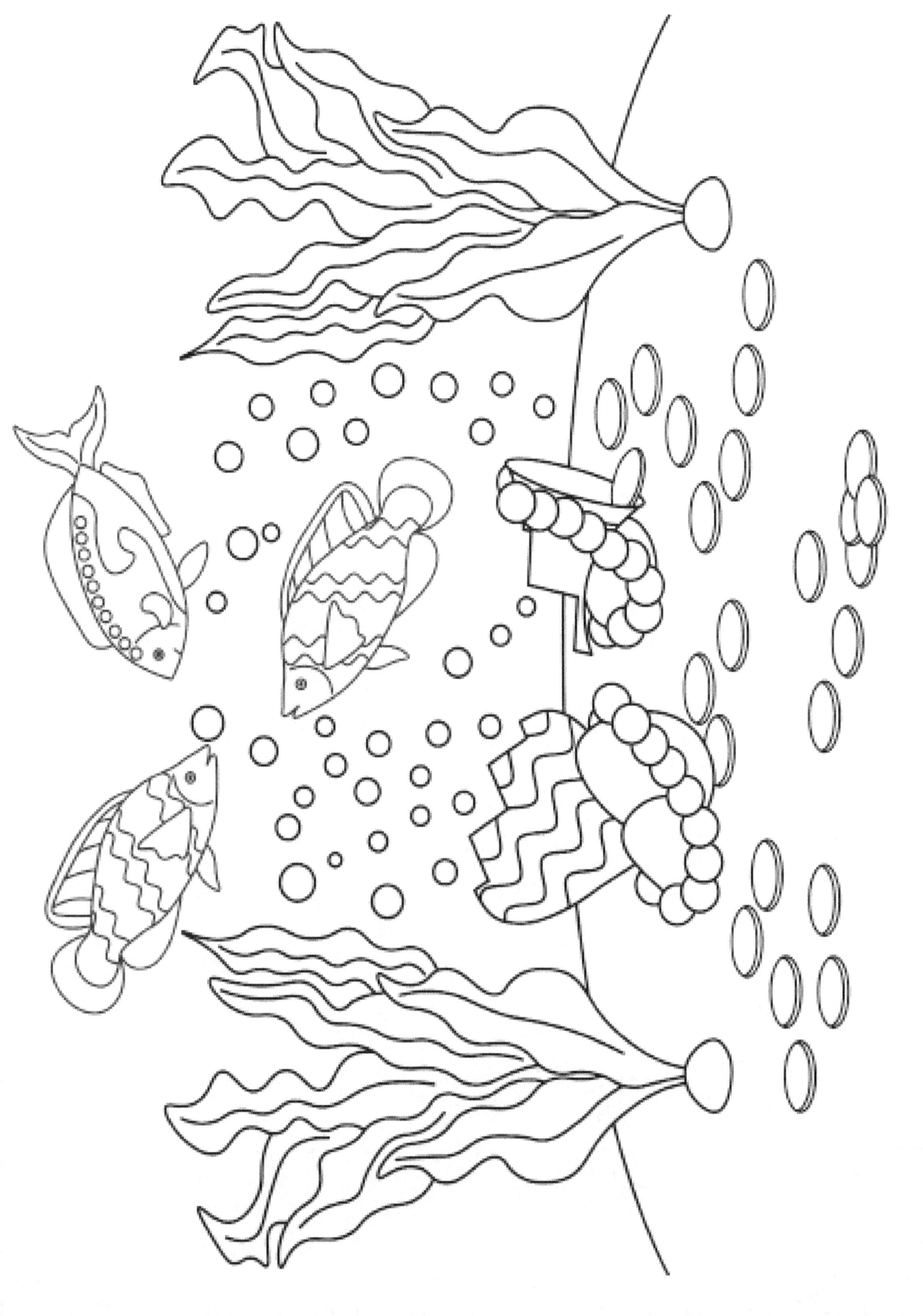

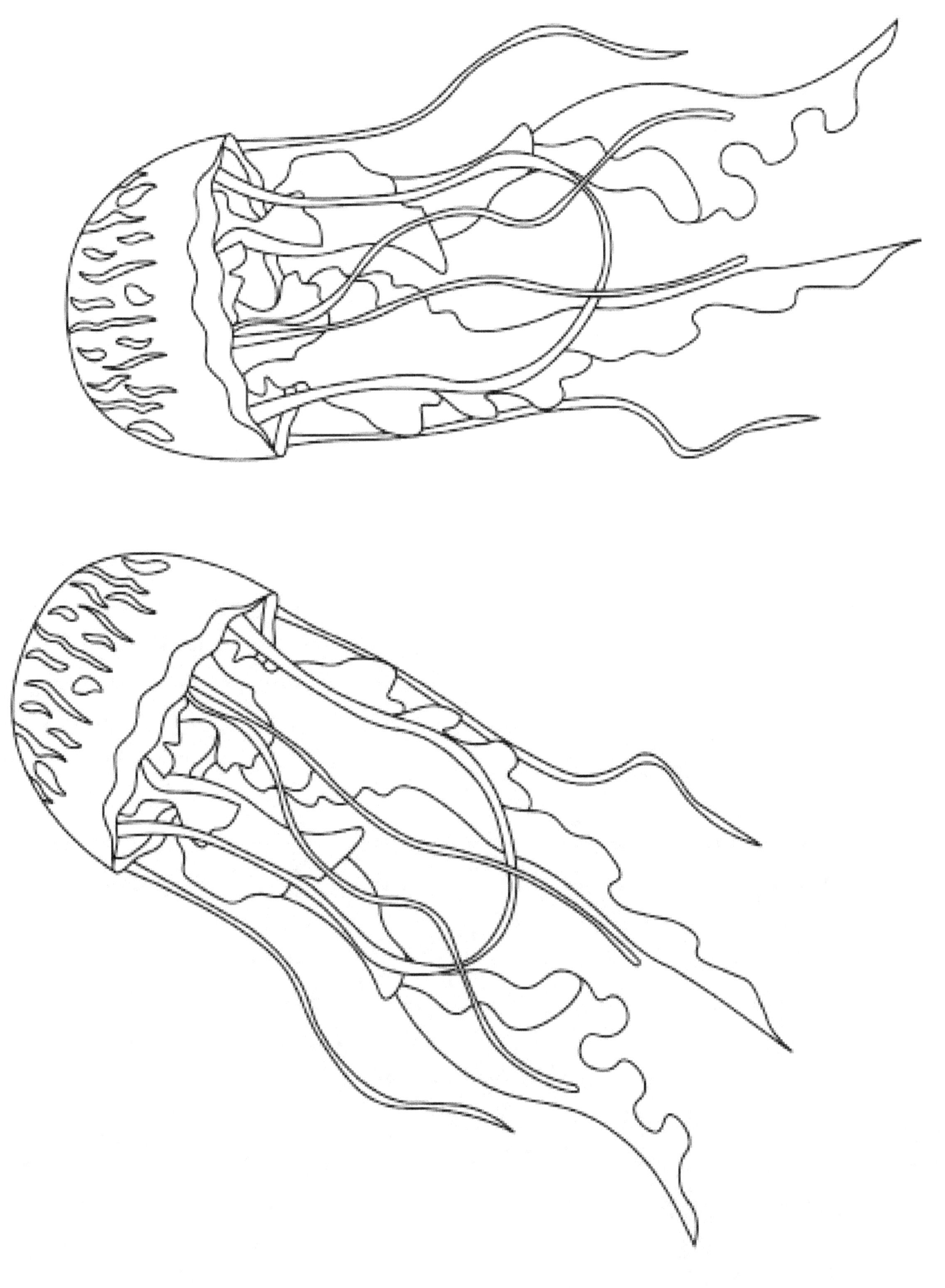

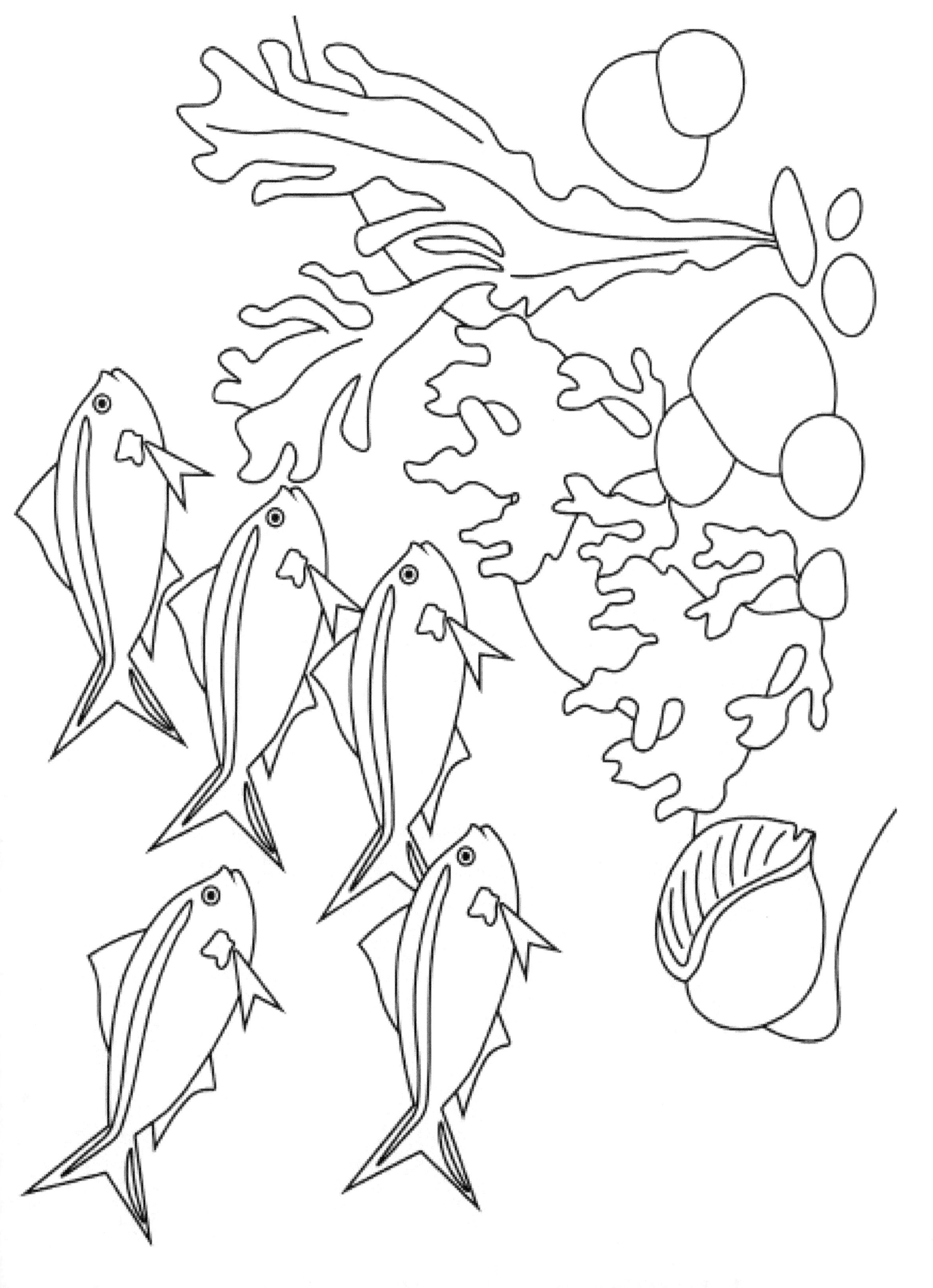

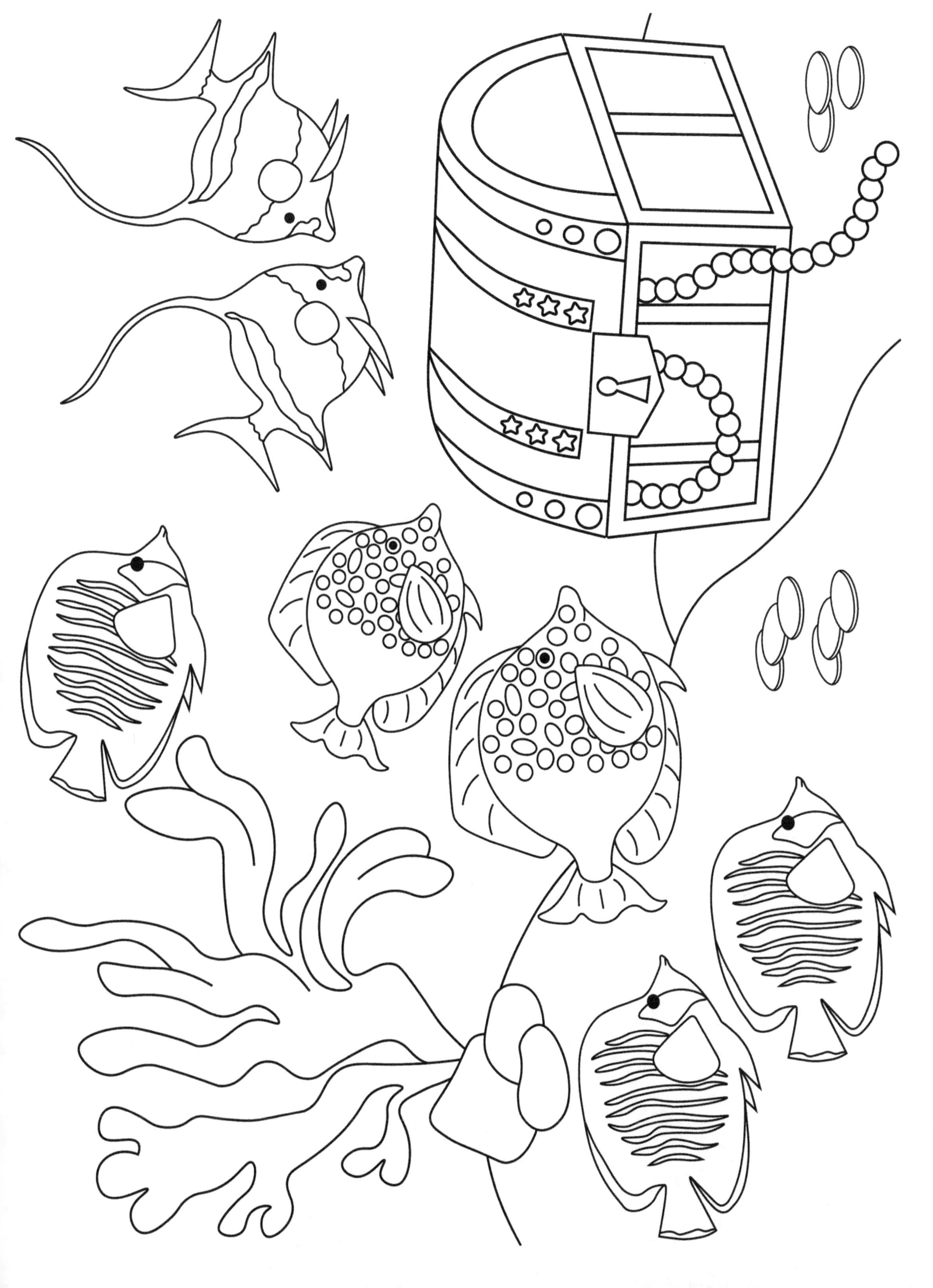

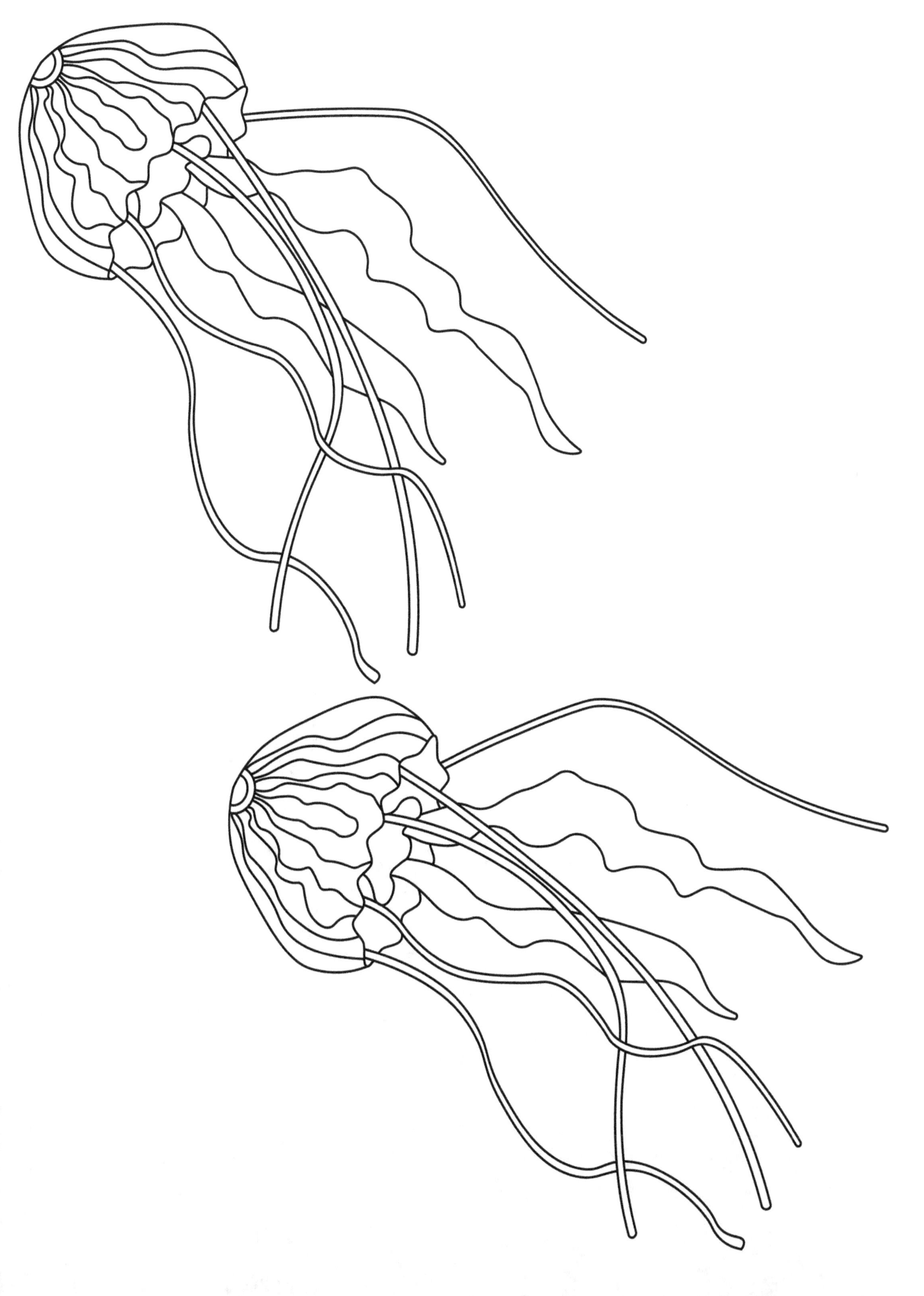

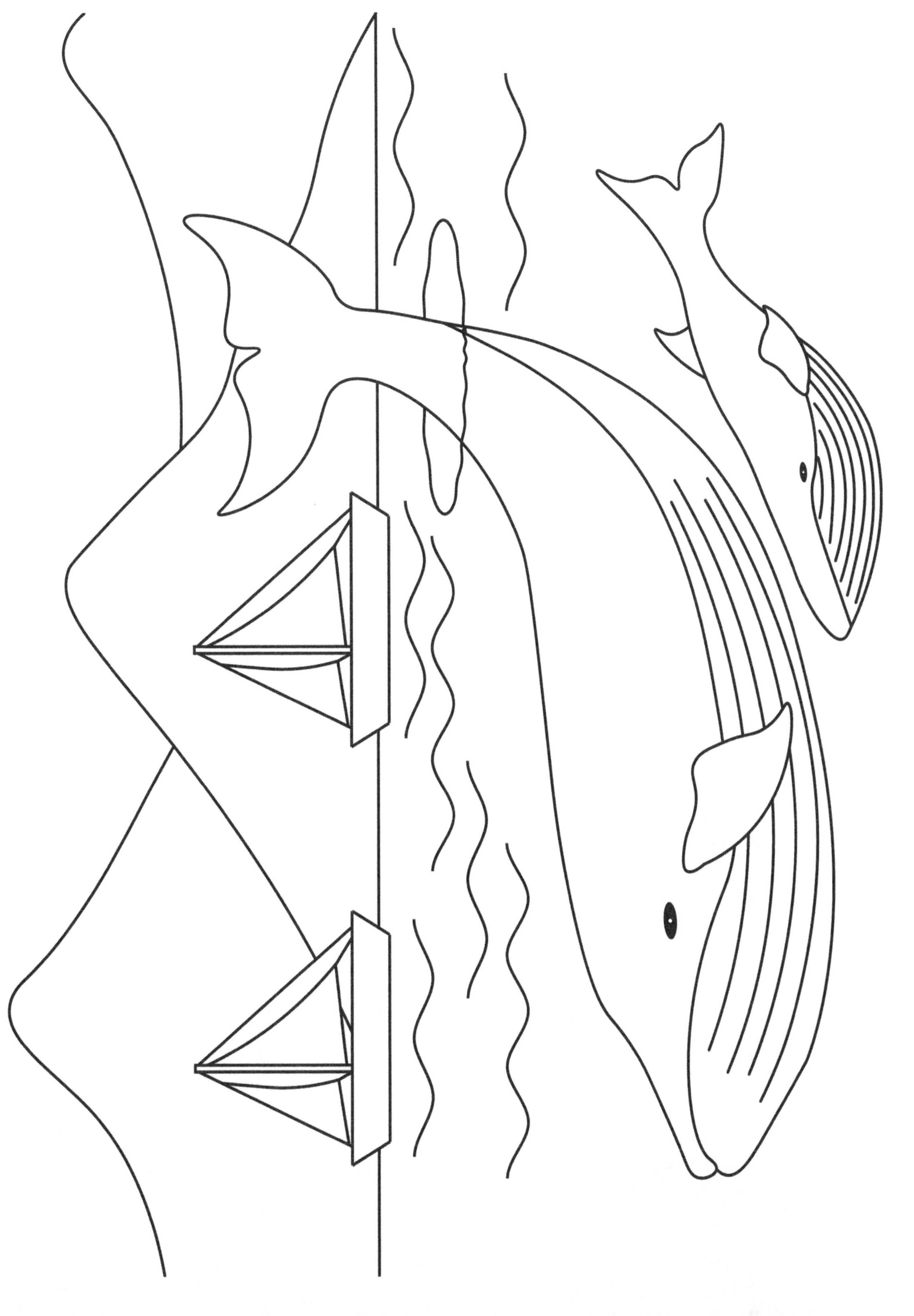

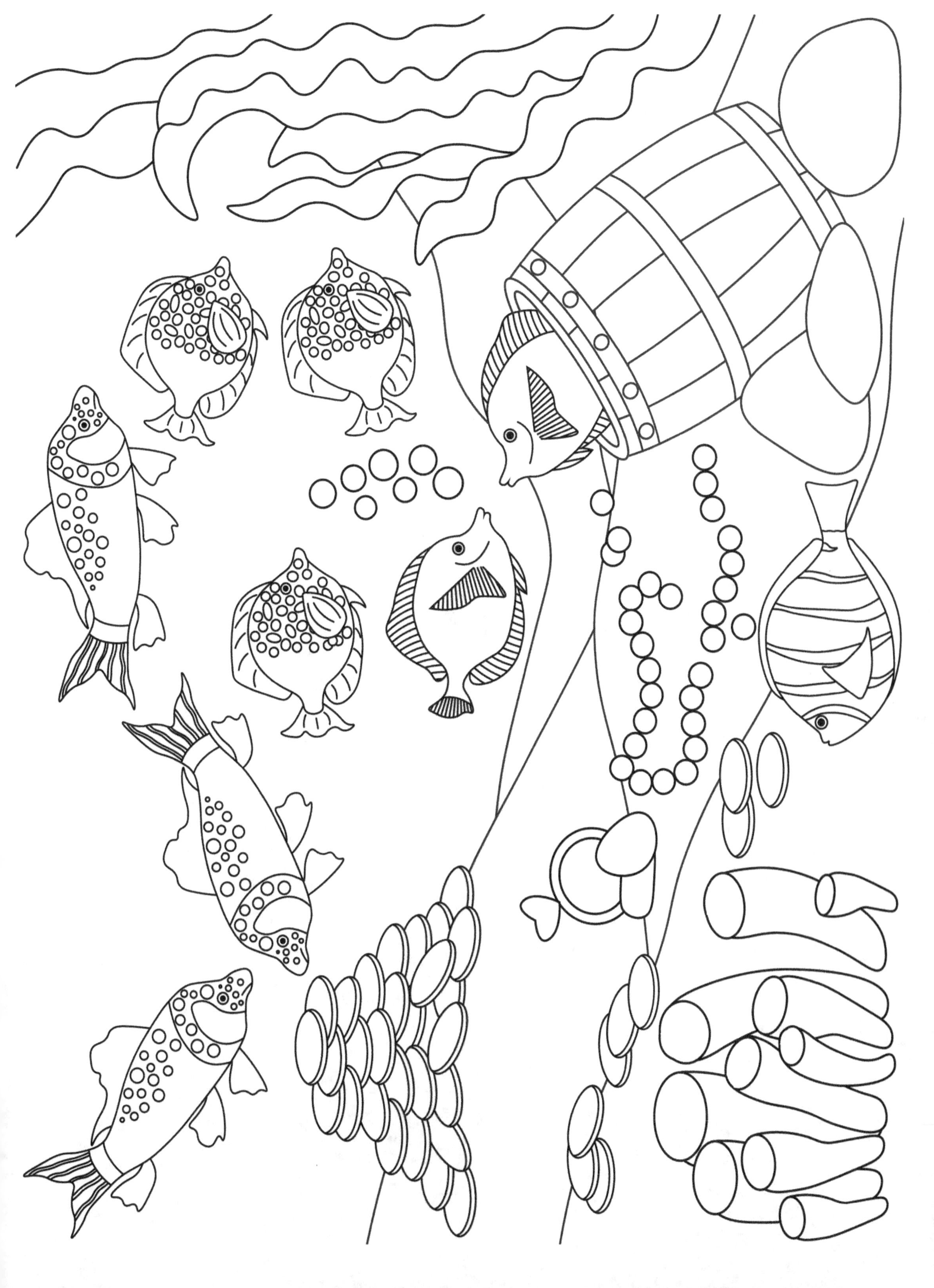

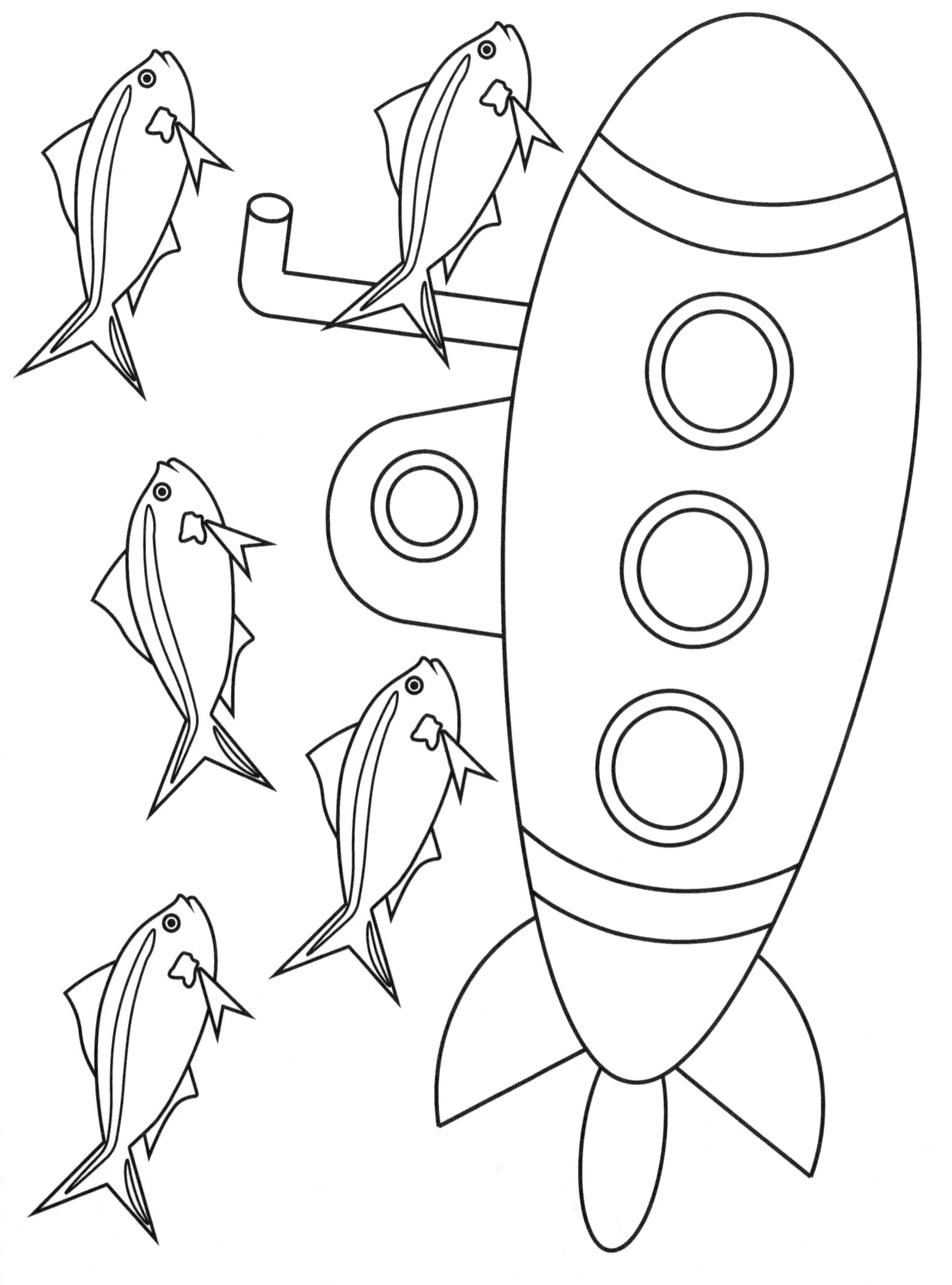

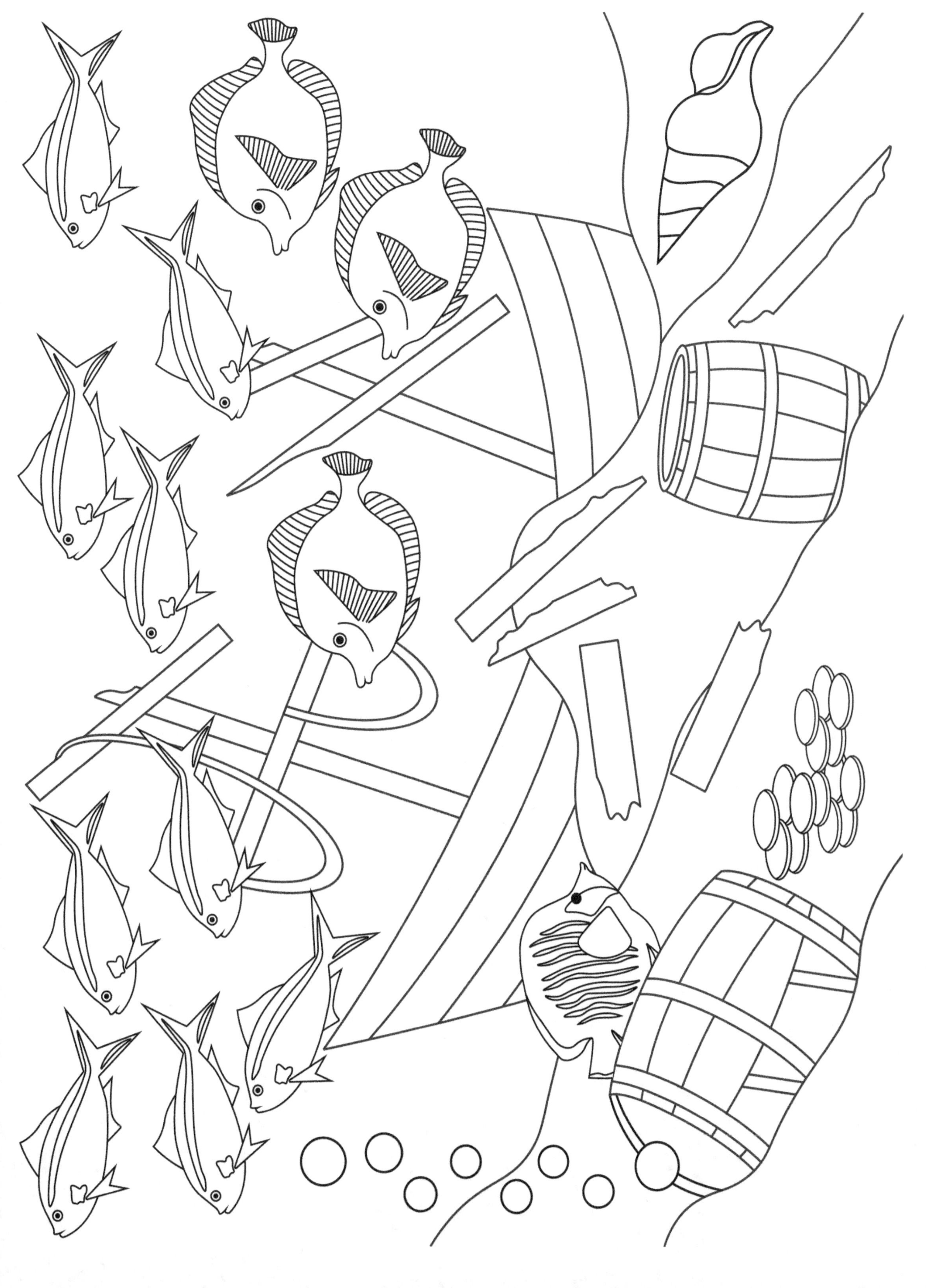

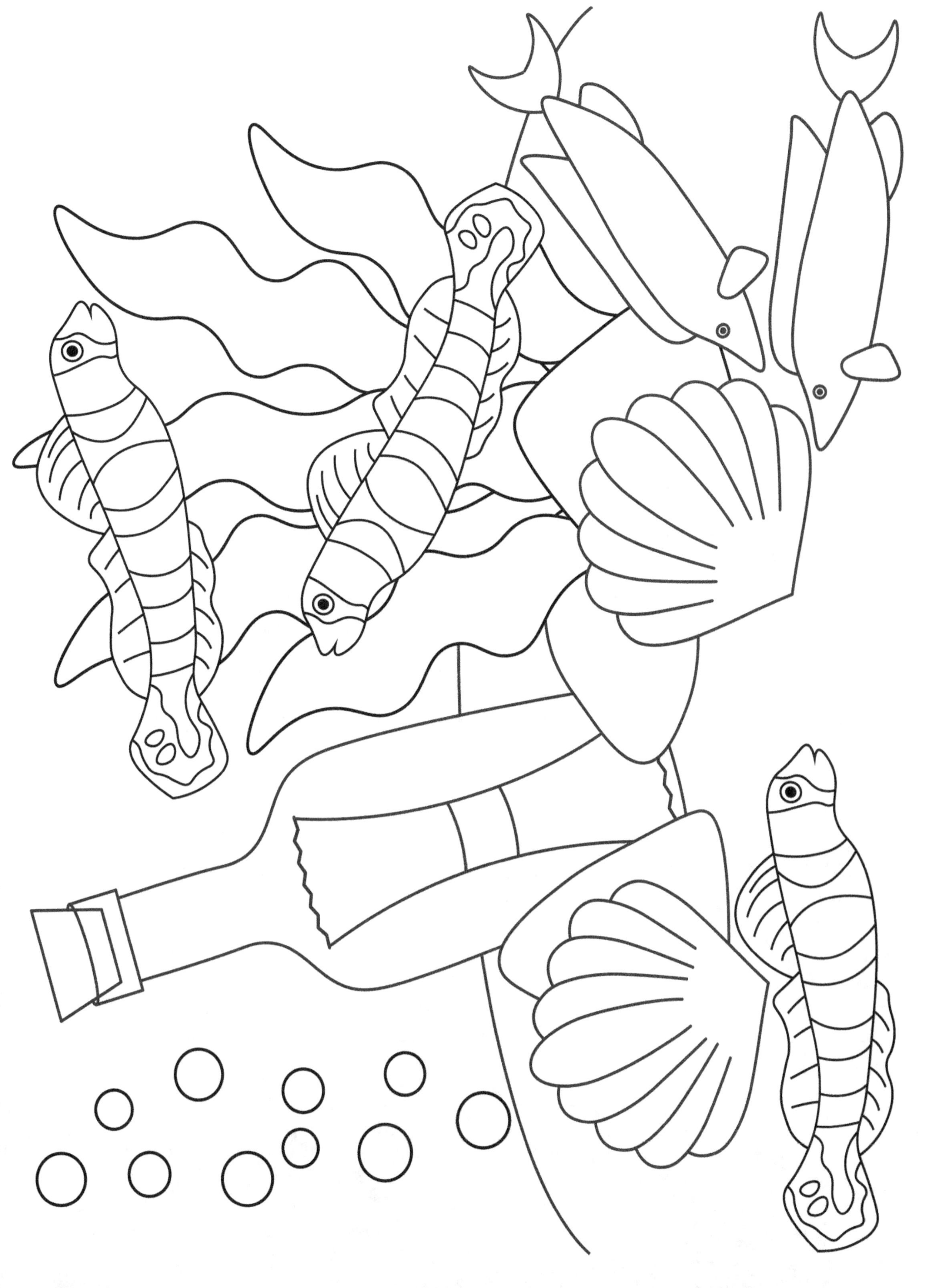

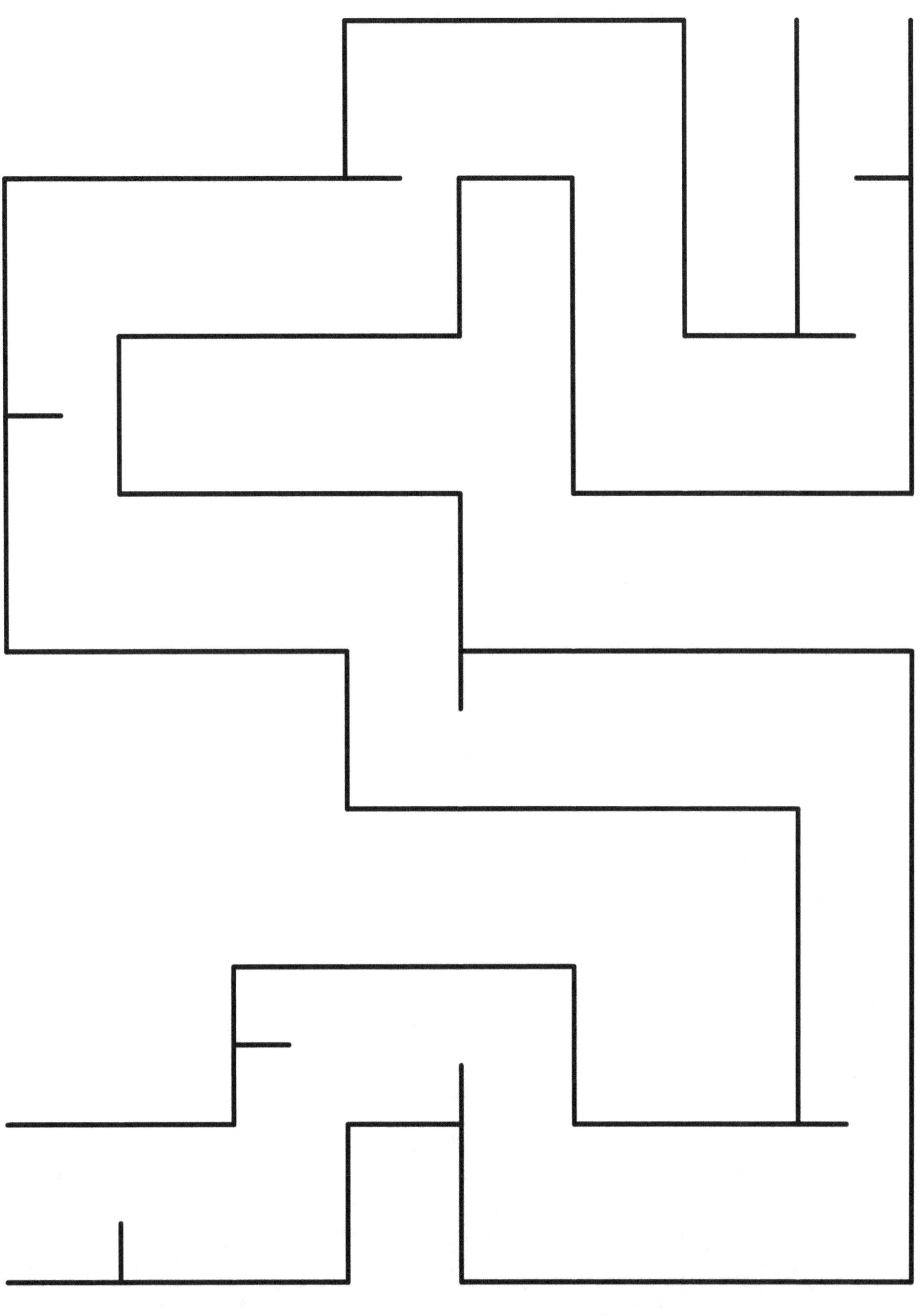

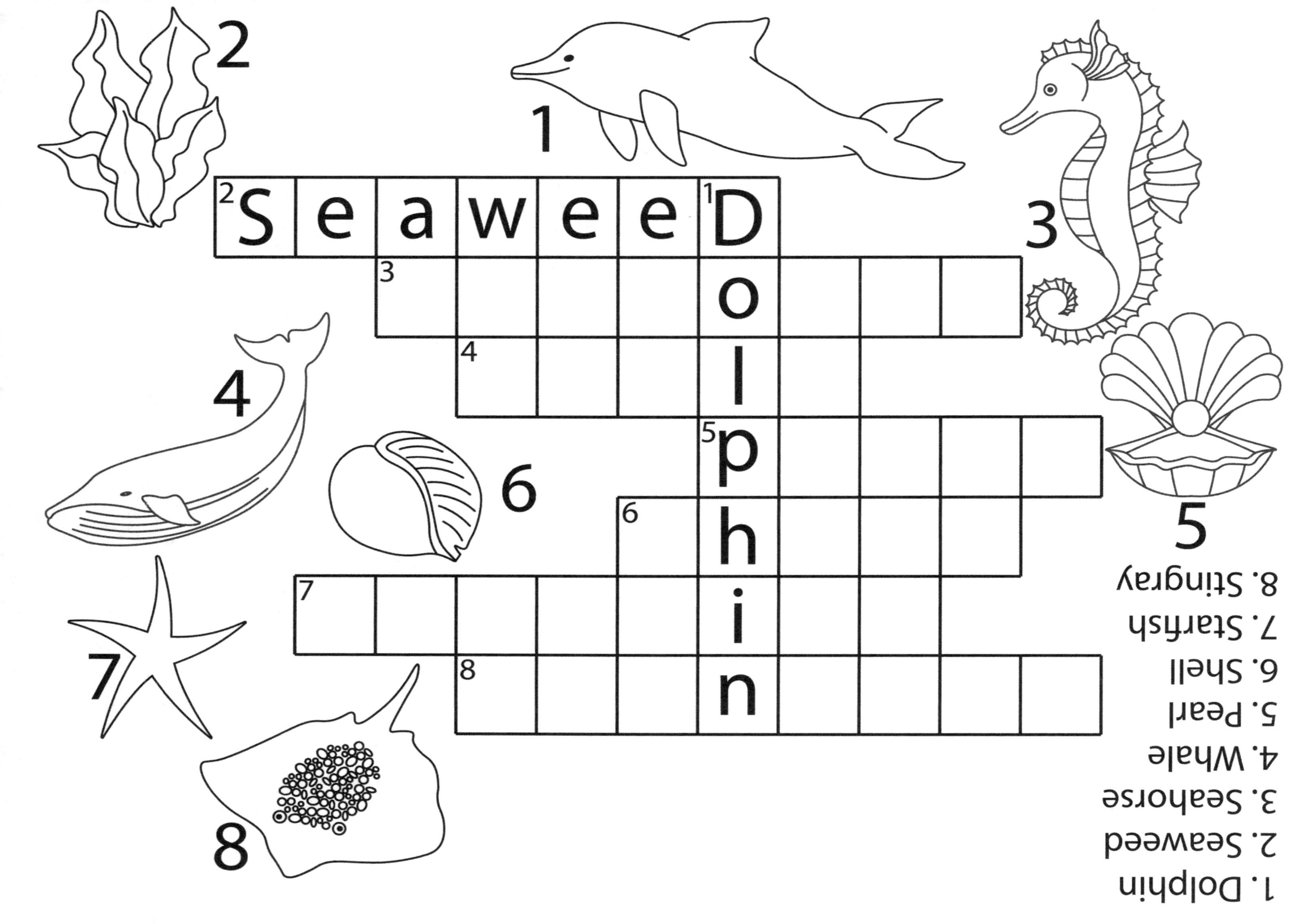

1. Dolphin
2. Seaweed
3. Seahorse
4. Whale
5. Pearl
6. Shell
7. Starfish
8. Stingray
Seaweed
Dolphin

www.ingramcontent.com/pod-product-compliance
Lightning Source LLC
Chambersburg PA
CBHW081427250726

48654CB00013B/1854